Hope
Has / Come

Hope
Has / Come

An Advent Devotional

Jayne Martin Patton

REDEMPTION PRESS

Published by Redemption Press, PO Box 427, Enumclaw, WA 98022.

Toll-Free (844) 2REDEEM (273-3336)

Redemption Press is honored to present this title in partnership with the author. The views expressed or implied in this work are those of the author. Redemption Press provides our imprint seal representing design excellence, creative content, and high quality production.

ISBN 13: 978-1-64645-098-5 (Paperback)
978-1-64645-102-9 (ePub)
978-1-64645-103-6 (Mobi)

Library of Congress Catalog Card Number: 2020923317

Introduction

Advent. A time of remembrance and of expectation. A season to recall the arrival of Jesus Christ as a baby over two thousand years ago. A moment to look forward with a heart full of anticipation to His return as King.

When Jesus was born, hope was restored to a people who had not heard from God in over four hundred years. His people needed to know He was still present when everything looked grim. The same is true for us. When we come to the end of a year and are looking back over the tumult we may have endured, it is powerful to remind ourselves that because of Jesus, God is *with* us. Just as Isaiah 7:14 prophesied, "She will give birth to a son and will call him Immanuel (which means 'God is with us')." This means:

In the day-to-day life, God is with us.

In the darkness of night, God is with us.

In the changing seasons, God is with us.

In the sadness, God is with us.

In the celebrations, God is with us.

In the breakups, God is with us.

In the restorations, God is with us.

It is necessary that we remind our children, our friends, and our nation that because of Jesus Christ, no matter the darkness we may have previously lived in, or are experiencing now, our futures can be bright! God is *with* us.

INTRODUCTION

So join us as we experience and explore the most incredible story ever told—the Advent story. Jesus came, and He is coming again. This is our living hope, and His name is Jesus.

Day 1

Many people have set out to write accounts about the events that have been fulfilled among us. They used the eyewitness reports circulating among us from the early disciples. Having carefully investigated everything from the beginning, I also have decided to write an accurate account for you, most honorable Theophilus, so you can be certain of the truth of everything you were taught.
Luke 1:1–4

Have you ever wanted to know something for yourself? Maybe you'd heard about it or read about it, but deep down you weren't quite convinced until you had researched on your own.

This is where we find our author, Luke. While he didn't have an eyewitness account of the events that occurred in Jesus's life, Luke had access to people who did. In these verses, he says that he investigated claims and met with sources regarding the extraordinary story of the birth of Jesus. After becoming personally convinced of its truth, he decided to ensure that the story was documented correctly for those who would come after him. Perhaps he thought if he wrote it clearly enough, others would believe and become followers of Jesus too.

It makes sense to me why he would do this. I think any time we've become completely convinced of the credibility of something, we want to persuade everyone else of its truth too.

Luke knew. Like, he *knew*. He knew this man Jesus was the real deal, and he communicated the greatest story that has ever been.

The most incredible story. The most life-impacting one. The story of a Man who still holds the ability to change the eternal future of every single person who will be convinced of it.

Join me for the next twenty-five days as we follow Luke's account of the most powerful story ever told. The Advent story—the story of the coming of Jesus Christ. I think you will discover, as Luke did, that because of the birth of Jesus, we will never again have to walk in hopelessness.

Day 2

*In the sixth month of Elizabeth's pregnancy, God sent the angel
Gabriel to Nazareth, a village in Galilee, to a virgin named Mary.*

Luke 1:26–27

God sent the angel Gabriel. . . . Stop and ponder this supernatural event. God is real, and in His very real heaven, He sends
very real angels to do His bidding. Sometimes I wonder how He
determines what sort of messages are deserving of an angel's delivery. I suppose, if anything, the announcement of His Son being
conceived would certainly qualify.

Interestingly, the angel Gabriel describes himself to Zacharias,
Elizabeth's husband, in Luke 1:19 as one who "stands in the presence
of God." The Greek word for "stands" is *paristánō*, which means to
wait before a superior.[1] It's the same word to describe how Joshua
served Moses and how David assisted King Saul. It seems Gabriel
repeatedly operates in the role of a messenger since his first biblical
appearance was in Daniel 8:16 when he explained a vision given to
the prophet Daniel.

We aren't told much about Gabriel's appearance, but we can
assume it was probably frightening. I surmise this because Daniel
was afraid when Gabriel appeared to him (Daniel 8:17). But Gabriel
was quick to offer comforting words to others he appeared in front
of. We see several examples in the Bible, especially surrounding
the news of Jesus's coming. When Gabriel first greets Zacharias, he

says, "Don't be afraid" (Luke 1:13). And while Mary's greeting is more celebratory, as he commends her that she "has found favor with God" (Luke 1:30), Gabriel also comforts her to not fear. With Gabriel's signature greeting, doesn't it make you wonder about what this angelic being looked like?

I suppose the important thing is not so much what he looked like as what he represents to us today. To me, Gabriel serves as a sweet example that God will do whatever it takes to communicate with His people. If He needs to communicate an extremely important message, He's not above speaking through an angelic messenger who stands in His presence waiting to do His bidding. I'm also challenged to consider if I wait on the Lord as much as the angels do. Am I standing in the presence of God waiting for my daily assignments? Gabriel may be an angel we read about and are mesmerized by, but he also serves as an inspiration of what it looks like to have total commitment to God. Today I am doing a heart check, standing and waiting for the assignments God has for me. Are you?

Thoughts about Advent

What do you think it would be like to receive a message from God from an angel today? Do you think God still does this? Why or why not?

Do you find yourself waiting in the presence of God for His assignments?

How can you position your heart to receive the work that He has for you today?

_____

_____

_____

_____

_____

_____

Day 3

She was engaged to be married to a man named Joseph, a descendant of King David.

Luke 1:27

Engaged. What an exciting word! It's a moment that many women look forward to, daydreaming about a beautiful location, a perfect man down on one knee, and a sparkling diamond ring to seal the deal; however, that's not exactly how Mary and Joseph's engagement would have gone down. In fact, it was more likely that this was an arranged marriage, as was fitting for the culture at that time. And this engagement? It was more like a formal contract between two families. So it was perhaps not as romantic as we'd like to think.

And yet here's the crazy thing about this whole arrangement: Mary couldn't be engaged to just anyone—it had to be someone who had the exact ancestors that Joseph had. As you read in this passage, Mary's soon-to-be groom was a descendant of King David. Why would this be such a big deal? Because Jesus had been prophesied to come through King David's lineage in 2 Samuel 7:11–16 and Isaiah 9:7. Friends, that this marital agreement had been made between these two families was *not an accident*. Whether they knew it or not, they were part of a divine orchestration that could have only come from God.

Why should this matter to us? Well, have you ever felt like some decisions were made for you without your opinions being considered? I have. And while I don't know if Mary had an opinion about Joseph—good or bad—prior to their engagement, it brings us peace to know that God is powerful enough to be working out *His* good plans in our lives even without our consent.

I think if we were being honest, we could admit that we often tell God exactly how we would like our lives to be orchestrated. We don't want any engagements we haven't approved of, nor do we want any decisions made for us without our consent. But the reality is God is wise enough to direct our lives without needing our opinions on creating the life we are meant to live.

We'll never know exactly how Joseph and Mary felt when they were first together, but I'd be willing to bet by the end of their lives, they were so glad they trusted God and went ahead with it.

Thoughts about Advent

Have you ever felt like decisions were being made about your life without being asked your opinion? How did that work for you?

How does it make you feel knowing you can trust God with your life even when you feel like you're being forced to *engage* in situations beyond your control?

_____

_____

_____

_____

_____

_____

Day 4

*Gabriel appeared to her and said, "Greetings, favored woman! The
Lord is with you!" Confused and disturbed, Mary tried to think
what the angel could mean.*
Luke 1:28–29

Can you imagine an angel showing up in your life? You're
just going right along, living your best life and then, bam! A supernatural being from heaven, who historically had the reputation of
terrifying people with his appearance, physically manifests himself
and starts speaking to you, calling you "favored," telling you that
"the Lord is with you." I don't know about you, but "confused and
disturbed" would have been the least of the descriptions used to
describe me. "Literally freaking out" would serve as a better descrip-
tion if it had been me.

Honestly? It's not hard to imagine that our friend Mary was
probably glued in place with her thoughts racing as rapidly as her
heart. *Is this real? What is even happening right now?*

The truth is, we may never have an encounter with an angelic
being, but the Lord still knows the exact ways to get our attention.
Whether it's through His Spirit, a person, a book, a sermon, the
Bible, a song, nature, whatever, the Lord still knows the most effec-
tive ways to communicate with us. Our job is to make sure we are
listening closely for His voice no matter how He chooses to speak.
His desire is that we not miss whatever He wants to say to us. As

it was with Mary, may we not be confused and disturbed when we hear His voice but trust God to make things clear to us in His time.

Thoughts about Advent

How has God chosen to speak to you recently? What has He spoken to you about? Write down your thoughts, and take them to the Lord if you need further direction. God's plans can be trusted, even if they aren't completely understood at first.

_____

_____

_____

_____

_____

_____

Day 5

"Don't be afraid, Mary," the angel told her, "for you have found favor with God!"

Luke 1:30

I don't know if we completely understand what it is to "have found favor with God." Looking at Mary's life, we discover that being favored by God would have included facts like:

- Poverty
- An unexpected teen pregnancy
- Giving birth in a barn
- Living under a cloud of questioning regarding her character and chastity for the remainder of her days
- Having more children who didn't originally believe her and Joseph about who Jesus really was
- Experiencing sleeplessness and anxiety-filled nights on the run
- Understanding that because of the birth of her own Son, other mothers would soon hold their own son's slaughtered and lifeless bodies in their arms
- Escaping to another country where she didn't know the language or the culture
- Knowing the loss of a husband and father to her children at some point before Jesus's death

- Feeling a mother's pain at seeing her perfect child betrayed, bullied, and then crucified on a cross

And yet God allowed all of this to one He considered "highly favored and blessed," and during all of this, God's perspective of what was good never changed. His opinion of Mary never changed. His choice of her, His favor toward her, His plans for her, as hard as they would be to bear, never affected His heart of blessing upon her life.

His goodness has me thinking that we ought not consider only the good times in our lives as blessed. Nor should we automatically think that we are somehow *lacking favor* from God during hard times. As we can see from Mary's life, receiving God's favor isn't always going to look exactly the way we think it should look. No matter what happens in our lives—good or bad—because Jesus is with us, God is for us, the Holy Spirit lives in us, and we are favored. Moreover, because the Lord will never leave us nor forsake us, we are blessed. And as it was for Mary, may the litmus test of our position before God be determined in His words *about* us, not by *what* we are experiencing. In good or bad times, those of us in Christ truly are highly favored and remain greatly blessed.

Thoughts about Advent

How have you previously defined *blessed by God*? Have you thought that only good things were blessings and bad things were not? Have you ever experienced something that looked bad but actually turned out to be a blessing from God? What ways can you trust God more?

_____

_____

_____

_____

_____

_____

Day 6

You will conceive and give birth to a son, and you will name him Jesus.

Luke 1:31

Names have always mattered. When naming our children, we might christen them with names from respected family members, attempt to honor a familial tradition or culture, or simply choose their name because we like the sound of it. The choice of Jesus's name revealed His mission. In fact, the name *Jesus* is the Greek form of "Joshua," which means "the Lord saves," and the Hebrew root word means to "rescue or deliver."[2]

Jesus's name also holds power. Jesus Himself said of it, "You can ask for anything *in my name*, and I will do it, so that the Son can bring glory to the Father. Yes, ask me for anything *in my name*, and I will do it!" (John 14:13–14, emphasis added). He also said to His disciples that "you will ask the Father directly, and he will grant your request because *you use my name*. You haven't done this before. Ask, *using my name*, and you will receive, and you will have abundant joy" (John 16:23–24, emphasis added). What other name could we possibly bring to God that would invoke such a positive response? God made it clear from the moment of His birth, the name of Jesus was one that would usher us into His presence and open up doors that had previously been shut.

You see, Jesus's name wasn't random. God gave it to Him on purpose because it held purpose, and still does. Jesus is still saving, still rescuing, and still delivering. His name is *still the name* that we ask in for all things. As the Apostle Paul said in Philippians 2:9, it is *still the name above all names*. It is *still the name* that every knee on the earth and under the earth will one day bow to. It is *still the name* that every tongue *will* declare is Lord over all.

Names matter, but Jesus's name is the one that matters most.

Thoughts about Advent

How has Jesus's name impacted your prayer life? How have you prayed previously in the name of Jesus, and how will it impact your future prayers?

_____

_____

_____

_____

_____

_____

Day 7

He will be very great and will be called the Son of the Most High.
The Lord God will give him the throne of his ancestor David.

Luke 1:32

Let me begin by assuring you, God keeps His promises.
Even when they feel like they are taking forever in coming, His promises will come to pass. This passage tucked in the first chapter of Luke was a fulfillment of God's promise to King David centuries earlier in 2 Samuel 7:16. Interestingly, when King David was given the promise of a descendant who would sit on his throne for all eternity, his response was a prayer of thanks. He ended with, "For you have spoken, and when you grant a blessing to your servant, O Sovereign Lord, it is an eternal blessing!" (2 Samuel 7:29). King David understood that while he may not see the promise come true in his lifetime, the blessings God gives will always have eternal impact.

In today's passage Gabriel confirmed to Mary that her newborn Son was indeed the prophesied descendant of King David that would assume his throne. The time had come. The promise was fulfilled. God had kept His Word.

Why does this matter to us today? Because there are some promises God will give us that, like King David before us, we may not see fulfilled in our lifetimes.

But the delay doesn't negate the promise!

We must stop thinking that God will bring about His will for the entire impact of our lives within our own temporal timeframes. Just like waiting until Christmas morning to receive a long-awaited gift, there are some packages the Lord is holding onto until just the right moment for us to unwrap. God is accomplishing a mighty work in our lives and has a perfect timetable for every detail. He isn't just interested in blessing us here and now. Rather, He is working on the details that will bless us for eternity.

Friends, don't be tempted to believe God will be unfaithful to you. Wait on Him even if it feels like it takes an eternity, because He can be trusted to fulfill His promises to you.

Thoughts about Advent

Have you ever felt like God was taking too long to fulfill a promise He made to you? Do you think He is to be trusted in light of eternity? In what areas can you reaffirm your trust in Him today?

_____

_____

_____

_____

_____

_____

Day 8

And he will reign over Israel forever; his Kingdom will never end!
Luke 1:33

Legend says that Roman Empire kings returning from a battlefield victory would have a slave to whisper in their ear as they paraded through the streets in celebration, "Sic transit Gloria Mundi," which is Latin for, "The glory of the world is fleeting," or "How quickly the glory of the world passes away." This phrase was to serve as a reminder that although they were experiencing the high of a great victory, future battles would be waged.

Similarly, Gabriel reminded Mary that in this earthly kingdom, nothing lasts forever. He essentially said to her, *No matter the heartbreak this situation may bring you, Mary, it is temporary. Keep your perspective. God is making a way for eternal joy to be made possible for all. It will all be worth it.* What she would see within her lifetime wouldn't reveal all that heaven held, so he encouraged her to keep her eyes focused on eternity.

That is hopeful news to those who are suffering; God's kingdom is eternal. It's a place where our joy will be complete and all of our hopes realized. A place where disappointment and sadness aren't allowed to exist. A place of perfect peace. A place where fear, pain, chaos, and death are no longer allowed to steal from us and where no hint of mourning exists. Mentioned several times in the New Testament, *this place* is what has been created for those of us who have accepted God's offer of salvation through Jesus Christ. This is God's kingdom, and Jesus is our hope.

Thoughts about Advent

Have you ever gotten caught up in thinking the heartache of this world is just too hard? Does it help you to consider that this isn't all there is? Of all the things there are to look forward to in God's kingdom, what is the number one thing you long to experience or see the most?

_____

_____

_____

_____

_____

_____

Day 9

Mary asked the angel, "But how can this happen? I am a virgin."
Luke 1:34

Mary had a valid question. Overwhelmed by the prospect of Gabriel's proclamation, she wanted to know, *How in the world will this impossible thing happen?* If we're honest, I think many of us still have similar questions today:

"But how can someone ever marry me again? I have
   been rejected by two husbands."
"But how can I ever go to college? I am broke."
"But how can I ever get that position? I don't have
   a degree."
"But how can that door ever be opened to me? I don't
   know the right people."
"But how can I ever write that book? I'm too old."
"But how can I ever obtain that level of respect? I'm
   too young."
"But how can I ever get on that stage? I'm bad at public
   speaking."
"But how can I ever take that first step toward freedom
   from abuse? I'm too afraid."

Friend, there is no *but how* in our lives that God does not have the answer to or is not the answer for. The God who made it possible for a virgin to conceive a baby is the same God who makes impossible things possible for you too.

We would do well not to rehearse all the reasons why we think God *cannot* do something, but instead we would do very well to meditate on His unlimited power to do *whatever* He desires to do.

If you're facing impossible odds today, meditate on the Scriptures that remind us that "with God everything is possible" (Matthew 19:26) and that He is able to do "far more abundantly than all that we ask or think" (Ephesians 3:20 esv). Our understanding of God's power will increase and our trust that He has the ability to accomplish all His plans for our lives will deepen. God *is* the *how*.

Thoughts about Advent

Have you ever questioned God with a *but how?* How does knowing that God is still doing the impossible change your thoughts? What are you trusting Him for today?

_____

_____

_____

_____

_____

_____

Day 10

The angel replied, "The Holy Spirit will come upon you, and the power of the Most High will overshadow you. So the baby to be born will be holy, and he will be called the Son of God."
Luke 1:35

Sometimes I wish the Bible expanded just a little bit more on some of the experiences that people had with God. Don't you wonder, even just a little bit, what it must have felt like for Mary when the Holy Spirit came upon her? What was she thinking when the power of the Most High overshadowed her? I mean, do we just imagine that she had this encounter with an angel, went to bed, and woke up pregnant? I don't know anyone outside of Adam who slept right through an experience with the living God. What I wouldn't give for a small peek into that moment.

I suppose what God does tell us about it, however, is sufficient. He wanted us to know that the Holy Spirit came upon her in such a way that she conceived Jesus. It's vital that we understand that this happened, even without all the step-by-step details, because it's an integral piece to the Christian faith. Everything about our faith rises and falls on this moment. Jesus was to be born both fully divine and fully man. My *NLT Study Bible* puts it this way: "Because Jesus was born of a woman, He was a human being, but as the Son of God, Jesus was born without any trace of human sin. Jesus was born both fully human and fully divine."

Jesus came with the power and authority to deliver people from their sins. A fully human man, born with a sin nature, could not accomplish this. Jesus as a human understands our thoughts, temptations, desires, and emotions. Hebrews 4:15 reminds us that "this High Priest of ours understands our weaknesses, for he faced all of the same testings we do, *yet he did not sin*" (emphasis added). Why is this important? Because Jesus as God knows how to deliver us from the sins that those thoughts, temptations, desires, and emotions lead us into. God knew we needed a fully man *and* a fully divine person to understand and rescue us.

There is a peace in knowing that because of His own humanity, Jesus fully understands our struggles. Because He experienced the same temptations we face and yet did not yield to them gives us hope that we can overcome our struggles with His Spirit living in us. Even today He calls out to us, letting us know that there is freedom from sin that can only be found in Him.

Thoughts about Advent

How does it make you feel to know that Jesus totally understands your struggles? In what areas do you need His divine deliverance today?

_____

_____

_____

_____

_____

Day 11

What's more, your relative Elizabeth has become pregnant in her old age! People used to say she was barren, but she has conceived a son and is now in her sixth month.

Luke 1:36

People talked about Elizabeth. They "used to say she was barren." Perhaps people talk about you too?

People used to say you were an addict.
People used to say you were lazy.
People used to say you were a gossip.
People used to say you used people to get ahead.
People used to say you couldn't keep a husband.
People used to say you were a drunk.
People used to say you got around.
People used to say you wouldn't amount to anything.

But here's the truth. All of that *used to* chatter came to a screeching halt when God intervened in your life. Yes, you and I may not be proud of all that we *used to be*, but that's just not who we are anymore.

So let people talk.

And in turn, let's give them the same response Paul gave in 1 Timothy 1:15–16, "This is a trustworthy saying, and everyone should accept it: 'Christ Jesus came into the world to save sinners'—and I am the worst of them all. But God had mercy on me so that Christ Jesus could use me as a prime example of His great patience with even the worst sinners. Then others will realize that they, too, can believe in Him and receive eternal life."

God is still the only One who can take who we used to be and turn us into who we were always meant to be.

Thoughts about Advent

What have people said about who you used to be? Since accepting Christ as your Savior, have you noticed any tangible changes regarding who you used to be and who you are now?

_____

_____

_____

_____

_____

_____

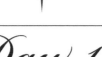

Day 12

For the word of God will never fail.
Luke 1:37

While Gabriel said many things to Mary during their encounter, this sentence alone remains one of the most powerful statements in the entire Bible. It makes me wonder why he told Mary that the Word of God would never fail. Do you think it was just a word of encouragement, or do you think maybe he knew she might be given to worry considering her new, miraculous circumstances? I believe it was said not solely to give her hope for the future but also to help her to remember God's unfailing words from the past.

Mary's own people, Abraham and Sarah, the parents of the Israelite nation, were also given a child by miraculous means. Sarah wasn't inclined to believe this would happen for her and God asked her a very pointed question in Genesis 18:14, "Is anything too hard for the Lord?"

When the angel asked Mary that question, he was asking her to remember what happened to Sarah. God's Word hadn't failed in the past; therefore, she could trust that it wouldn't fail her in the present.

Why is this important to us today? Because the Word of God is true, and nothing He says will fail you. From the beginning of time until today, the promises of God remain. We must continually remember that nothing is impossible for God and that everything

He speaks is still possible today. Friends, this means that you and I can still trust Him today.

Thoughts about Advent

How can you trust God with your situation right now? If you are unsure, what does His Word say to you as it applies to your situation? What are some of God's promises about you or your situation that you can begin believing?

_____

_____

_____

_____

_____

_____

_____

Day 13

Mary responded, "I am the Lord's servant. May everything you have said about me come true." And then the angel left her.

Luke 1:38

Mary is one of my favorites. I love talking about her because her life teaches us so much about how she handled the unexpected news of the coming Messiah. Her settled and calm response to Gabriel's news reveals her thoughts about the situation. She was committed to embracing whatever God had determined should occur, no matter the cost.

Mary's peaceful response just about boggles my mind. I can't tell you how many times when I have been given unexpected news that I've said, *Really, Lord? You've got to be kidding me. I'm not in, Lord, I'm so not in. In fact, I'm out!* I have the incredible ability to throw the most unholy fit when I want to.

But not Mary. She had questions, of course. What woman wouldn't? But her attitude to submit to whatever God had planned reveals something about her faith. She trusted God more than she was afraid. More than she needed all the facts up-front. More than she needed additional evidence. She simply trusted God.

When I receive unexpected news, I want to have the same response Mary had. I want my attitude to be settled on trusting God in advance of all the answers.

Don't you? Then let's commit to making the same willful declaration to God that Mary did: "May everything you have said about me come true." Especially as we learn how to respond correctly to the unexpected news that comes in our own lives.

Thoughts about Advent

Have you ever received unexpected news and wondered if God really does have a plan? How did you respond? How does it make you feel that nothing surprises God and that He has a plan for all of it?

_____

_____

_____

_____

_____

_____

Day 14

A few days later Mary hurried to the hill country of Judea, to the town where Zechariah lived. She entered the house and greeted Elizabeth.

Luke 1:39–40

Any time we are given unexpected news, we have decisions to make. I believe Mary's decision to visit Elizabeth has the ability to show us what to do when we are given unexpected news. Mary probably would have realized that she would be facing judgmental townspeople, flying rumors, and everyone offering their own opinions on her unusual situation.

So what did she do? Mary ran away from the outside distractions and straight to her cousin Elizabeth, who was a woman of God and a priest's wife. Mary hastened to someone she knew would believe her incredible story because she, too, had an incredible story. She went to Elizabeth, the woman Gabriel had revealed was impossibly pregnant in her old age. Mary knew out of anyone else, Elizabeth would most certainly understand.

What Mary did is critical to processing unexpected news. There is value in surrounding ourselves with other women of God who know and understand what we are going through. Even if your friends cannot possibly understand exactly what it is you are going through, the fact that they are pointing you to the character of God's goodness and faithfulness in the chaos is exactly what you need and is precisely what Elizabeth did for Mary.

There will be some things that happen in your journey where you are just going to have to walk by faith, whether people believe you or not. Not everyone is going to understand or embrace what you know God has spoken to you, and people don't have to for it to still to be true. Keep trusting Jesus no matter what.

You can't stem unexpected news, but you can learn how to process it. Like it was for Mary, perhaps it's time for you to tune out all the incoming voices and just surrender to the Lord's voice. Maybe you need to get away from all the distractions and seek out other godly women to surround yourself with. After all, when Mary did that, God used it to confirm her destiny. What will He confirm for you?

Thoughts about Advent

Do you tend to isolate yourself when you've been given unexpected news, or do you seek out others who have walked that road before you? What value can you see in seeking out wise friends in times of need? What distractions do you need to silence so you can seek God apart from the unexpected news you've been given?

_____

_____

_____

_____

_____

Day 15

At the sound of Mary's greeting, Elizabeth's child leaped within her, and Elizabeth was filled with the Holy Spirit. Elizabeth gave a glad cry and exclaimed to Mary, "God has blessed you above all women, and your child is blessed. Why am I so honored, that the mother of my Lord should visit me? When I heard your greeting, the baby in my womb jumped for joy. You are blessed because you believed that the Lord would do what he said."

Luke 1:41–45

Oh the comfort Mary must have felt in that moment after entering the house and hearing Elizabeth's response of overwhelming gladness at her arrival and confirming what Mary already knew to be true in her heart. I imagine that Mary was flooded with instant peace. Affirming words from other believers can often do that for us, can't they?

Elizabeth said Mary was blessed because she "believed that the Lord would do what He said." Mary was confident that God would be true to His Word. I think the same can be true for us. We must continually filter our emotions and our circumstances on God doing what He said He will do and trusting that God is who He says He is.

Some of the truths we can depend on God for are found squarely in His Word. They assure us that God knows things that we do not and that joy will come even if we are struggling with depression or hardships. We are reminded that God is our helper and we can call on Him any time we are in need or in trouble. God's

Word tells us that His love toward us is unconditional and does not waver based on what we've done or how far we've walked away.

Friends, we can *trust* that every single thing that touches our lives has first been filtered through God's loving hands and intentional purposes. Mary was blessed because she believed God at His Word. Do you want to be blessed? Believe for what the Lord has promised you. If you are unsure of His promises, go to His Word and ask Him to speak to you. If you are just starting out, you can even do a web search for "promises of God," make a list of them, meditate on them, and ask the Lord to show you when and where to apply them over your situations. You will find that the blessing will come, just as it did for Mary, when you believe that the Lord will do what He has said.

Thoughts about Advent

What is a promise God has given you that you are believing Him for? What is a promise you can see that He has already fulfilled? How do His promises give you hope for today?

_____

_____

_____

_____

_____

_____

Day 16

Oh, how my soul praises the Lord.
How my spirit rejoices in God my Savior!
For he took notice of his lowly servant girl,
and from now on all generations will call me blessed.
For the Mighty One is holy,
and he has done great things for me.
He shows mercy from generation to generation
to all who fear him.
His mighty arm has done tremendous things!
He has scattered the proud and haughty ones.
He has brought down princes from their thrones
and exalted the humble.
He has filled the hungry with good things
and sent the rich away with empty hands.
He has helped his servant Israel
and remembered to be merciful.
For he made this promise to our ancestors,
to Abraham and his children forever.

Luke 1:46–55

This passage is known as the Magnificat, or the "Song of Mary." Mary's song reveals she had no other response than praise in that moment! Her soul rejoiced that God had chosen her. Knowing that she hadn't done anything deserving of such an honor, she saw that God just chose to bless her out of His great love for her. She wasn't wealthy or positionally worthy of such an honor. Mary recognized what the majority of us miss. She saw God as One who moves among the lowly and humble of heart, not the arrogant and powerful, and as One who esteems both the elderly and the young. After all, Elizabeth and Mary weren't prestigious women. They weren't at the top of the Israeli social pyramid. They hadn't broken through some invisible religious stratosphere where some think God has reserved His most important work. Instead Mary could see that God was working in her young and poor life, and also in Elizabeth's elderly and barren life.

In her song, Mary was quick to identify why others would call her blessed. She knew it wasn't because she was chosen to be Jesus's mother; rather, she understood that it was based purely on God's holiness and His work in her life. Mary referenced multiple times that God is partial to those who fear Him and are humble.

Friends, it's so important that we understand this. We cannot quickly default to thinking we are blessed if our bank accounts are full, if we are without any real needs, or if we don't need to depend on anyone for anything. This thinking leads to a prideful heart, which God does not honor. Furthermore, God will always bless what man inherently resists: humility.

Like Mary, those of us in Christ weren't chosen because we earned the right to be chosen. He chose us because of His holiness. He chose us because He still desires to do great things both through and for us. His unending mercy remains today for you and for me and even for those who have hardened their hearts toward Him. His mighty arm is still stretched out toward us ready to do tremendous things.

He is waiting for us to return to Him today. Oh that we would humble ourselves and trust Him more. Let us never forget that everything good in our lives rises and falls on His holiness, not ours.

Thoughts about Advent

Knowing that God blesses us out of His holiness, how does that impact how you serve Him? How does it change the way you view how He sees and blesses people?

_____

_____

_____

_____

_____

_____

Day 17

Mary stayed with Elizabeth about three months and then went back to her own home. When it was time for Elizabeth's baby to be born, she gave birth to a son. And when her neighbors and relatives heard that the Lord had been very merciful to her, everyone rejoiced with her.

Luke 1:56–58

I have always heard that Mary stayed long enough to help Elizabeth give birth to the baby who grew to be John the Baptist. A quick study in biblical hermeneutics, however, brings forth the idea, albeit not conclusively, that Mary left prior to John's birth.

What was the reason behind Mary's staying for three months? Some scholars suggest it was for the benefit of Jewish doctors who, at that time, would use a three-month timeline to confirm pregnancy and determine paternity. For instance, they wanted to ensure that a woman wasn't pregnant by one man before being divorced and marrying another. Other theologians reinforce the idea that Mary stayed to understand the birthing process, and those three months served as a time of preparation for her.

I don't know why she stayed that long. Perhaps it was for reasons not clearly defined in Scripture. But what I do know is that for those three months, Mary and Elizabeth were two women committed to encouraging and believing God together for great miracles.

I wonder if they whispered over shared meals of what might become of their boys. Did they talk about how they would raise them to know and love God? Was Elizabeth concerned her husband might never speak again after being silenced by an angel for not believing his wife would have a son in her old age? Would it all fall on her shoulders to communicate the things of God? Did they discuss their fears over their future? Did they chat about how they were going to afford their new additions to the family? Did one encourage the other about what they had seen and experienced when other women gave birth?

We can't ever forget that these were real women with real concerns, emotions, fears, joys, and expectations. Perhaps Mary and Elizabeth were a gift to one another, and at the same time, perhaps God was doing something extraordinary in both of their hearts while they were together. As a woman, I can wholeheartedly say that there is something incredibly special about a friend who stays. Whether it's for a week, a month, three months, or longer, a friend who stays during life's most complicated seasons is simply a gift from God.

Thoughts about Advent

Have you ever experienced the gift of a friend who just stayed? What meant most to you through that experience? Has it changed how you minister to your friends?

_____

_____

_____

_____

_____

_____

✦

Day 18

At that time the Roman emperor, Augustus, decreed that a census should be taken throughout the Roman Empire. (This was the first census taken when Quirinius was governor of Syria.) All returned to their own ancestral towns to register for this census. And because Joseph was a descendant of King David, he had to go to Bethlehem in Judea, David's ancient home. He traveled there from the village of Nazareth in Galilee. He took with him Mary, to whom he was engaged, who was now expecting a child.

Luke 2:1–5

Caesar Augustus's name actually meant "exalted," and he was known for his military prowess. He was esteemed for having ended a long stretch of war in the Roman Empire and while he worshiped pagan gods, it's also recorded that he allowed himself to be worshiped as a living god. Under his rule, the economy grew as Rome was rebuilt, much out of Augustus's own personal wealth.

It's said there was peace in the empire, but the tragic reality was that Augustus slaughtered anyone he considered his enemy. His way of achieving peace was to suppress human rights and freedoms. If you were to receive the peace Rome was offering, you would need to submit to totalitarian rule. As Professor Elizabeth Johnson writes in her commentary on Luke 2:1–20, "Of course, peace achieved by coercion and oppression is no true peace at all."[3]

When Augustus decreed that a census should be taken, he was actually fulfilling a biblical prophecy issued some six hundred years before by the prophet Micah (Micah 5:2). While Augustus may have thought he was just organizing a census for tax purposes, God was using him to fulfill the prophecy of a ruler over Israel coming from Bethlehem. The Lord had a plan for true peace and would use those considered the most evil to accomplish it.

Don't miss the importance of what God did here. There will be times when we feel as though we have to submit to unjust rulers and unfair commands. There will be times that we have to surrender to bosses and leaders who seem to be making decisions to serve their own purposes. In these times, it is vital to remember that God is still working all things together for our good (Romans 8:28). We need to remember that while things might seem bleak, God's purposes will stand, and God's plans will be actualized.

When Caesar Augustus ruled, there was no real peace. That's why we needed the Prince of Peace to come. No matter how one-sided a situation may be, man still cannot thwart the plans of God. Friends, you can trust Him. When it seems like you are being ruled by unjust leaders, when it feels like governments are making terrible choices, when it looks like legislation is being written that you fundamentally oppose, or mandates are being given that you feel infringe on our freedoms, God is still working to fulfill His own plans through it all. His agenda will stand.

Thoughts about Advent

Have you ever felt like you were being ruled by unjust leaders? Did it make you wonder if God had lost control of the world? How does it make you feel that even in the worst of circumstances, God is still in control and working all things out together for good?

_____

_____

_____

_____

_____

Day 19

And while they were there, the time came for her baby to be born.

Luke 2:6

Did you know that the New Testament identifies two different concepts of time? The ancient Greeks used two separate words to describe time: *chronos* and *kairos*. *Chronos* is sequential by nature. It's best thought of in terms of calendars and clocks, and it's where we get the English word *chronological*. *Kairos* is more about the right season or occasion, which some Greek dictionaries define as the "right time, an opportune time, the proper time, or the appointed time."[4]

When Jesus came into the world, He came on *kairos* time. Right on time you could say, according to God's *chronos* timetable. Why care about these time differences and descriptions? Because God is still working within those two timetables. There are some things God will do in our lives that will fall within a *chronos* time frame and others within *kairos* time frame. For instance, have you ever felt like you've waited years for answered prayers, and other times answered prayers happen rapid fire? It's because God is using both time frames to accomplish His plans and purposes for us. When we don't receive an immediate answer, we can't default into thinking God isn't answering a prayer. While we want Him to respond on a *kairos* time frame, He may very well be intending on responding within a *chronos* time frame.

When Jesus came, God knew about the entire history of the Jewish people. He knew about the prophecies. He knew about the slavery. He knew about the unjust practices of the Roman Empire. And at just the *kairos* time on His *chronos* timetable, God sent Jesus.

This reassures me that God hasn't missed one prayer that you've offered up. He knows about your prodigal child. He knows about the diagnosis. He knows who sits in authority over you. He knows about your marriage. Not every answer to our prayers will happen within our desired time frames. You may think the Lord is responding too slowly, but I can assure you He will answer right on time.

Thoughts about Advent

Jesus was the answer to all of humanity's prayers, and He came at just the appointed time—*kairos* time. How does that make you feel about waiting on the answers to the prayers you've offered up? Does it make you worship God any differently this Christmas than before?

_____

_____

_____

_____

_____

_____

Day 20

*She gave birth to her firstborn son. She wrapped him snugly in strips
of cloth and laid him in a manger, because there was no lodging
available for them.*
Luke 2:7

When we read the words "firstborn son," our thoughts immediately envision a tiny and helpless infant. That would be correct, but if that's all we visualized, it would severely limit our understanding of who He really is. So who was Mary's firstborn son? I'm so glad you asked. This wasn't just a weak, little baby or insignificant child born in Bethlehem. No. This soft-skinned human babe who now lay in a feeding trough, protected only by strips of cloth, actually encompassed *all* the power, *all* the strength, *all* the knowledge, and *all* the peace that could possibly exist *ever*. Mary's firstborn child was literally God clothed in flesh.

Thinking back upon this unique birth, and knowing Mary and Joseph had no formal lodging, as all inns were at capacity, I have to believe that the innkeeper who rejected them simply had no clue what was happening in that stable. Because if he had, it would make any sane person wonder why he didn't drop everything, clear out all the other weary travelers, and make room for this very special delivery.

Interestingly, God didn't force the innkeeper to make room for the birth of His Son. True to His character, He won't force His way into the inns of our lives either. Just as it was for the innkeeper, God leaves the decision up to us to make room for Him. For unbelievers, God's invitation is always extended to receive Him as their personal Savior. And for believers, we also are given the invitation to continue to give Him access to every capacity of our lives.

We must ensure that we aren't too full of ourselves to make room for the Lord. We need to invite Him in to clear out the undesirable squatters, like fear and depression, that have forced their way into our inns. We need to allow God's Spirit to vacuum out the bitterness that has moved in. We need to give Him permission to sweep away unresolved anger and addictions that have been tearing up the sacred place in our soul. After all, these deceiving travelers have never paid one red cent, and yet we've struggled to kick them out.

I can't go back in time and persuade the innkeeper to let the Glory of the world into his inn, but I can invite you to let Jesus be the honored guest in yours. It will be the greatest decision you've ever made. He's known for giving complete upgrades to the earthly inns He's made His home, and you'll discover that He's a tenant who has already paid in full, up-front, for a lifetime.

Thoughts about Advent

Like the innkeeper, have you rejected Christ when He arrived at the door of your life, or have you made room for Him to stay? If you've invited Him in, have you given Him access to every room and invited Him to clean your inn of all the other undesirable tenants? If not, how can you do that today?

_____

_____

_____

_____

_____

Day 21

That night there were shepherds staying in the fields nearby, guarding their flocks of sheep. Suddenly, an angel of the Lord appeared among them, and the radiance of the Lord's glory surrounded them. They were terrified, but the angel reassured them. "Don't be afraid!" he said. "I bring you good news that will bring great joy to all people."
Luke 2:8–10

"Good news that will bring great joy to all people" was monumental information, not just because the Messiah had finally come but because He had come for *all* people. Even though the Lord chose shepherds to spread the glad tidings, and while many of the heroes of our faith had been shepherds (think Abraham, Isaac, Jacob, Moses, and David), by the time Luke was writing this summary, shepherds were not held in great respect. In fact, an ancient midrash on Psalm 23:2 reads, "There is no more disreputable occupation than that of a shepherd."[5] At the time of the announcement in Luke, shepherds weren't even allowed to serve in any type of judicial role or as any type of witness in court.

Why then would God have the angels give such wonderful news to people in a despised class? Was He, as some scholars believe, announcing that the former way of worship would no longer be required to those who were responsible for guarding the sheep required for sacrifice? Was God going out of His way to say that the perfect, sacrificial Lamb had finally come? Perhaps.

But maybe it was also as Dr. Ralph Wilson suggests that "perhaps this is because Jesus, who has fellowship with the despised and sinners, knew and appreciated them as people."[6] Jesus didn't look at the shepherds as individuals to be shunned but as those He dearly loved. Maybe that is also why God chose to make this incredible announcement to them first.

Jesus had a wild habit over His three years of ministry of showing up to those considered the "least of these" (Matthew 25:40). Over and over again in Scripture, He showed up to the marginalized, the broken, and the outcasts to bring them good news. He ministered and elevated women, He touched the lepers, He delivered the possessed.

There are probably many reasons why Christ's birth announcement was made the way it was and to whom it was made. But we see a pattern of Jesus reaching out to the least of these, which reveals His heart toward us. He didn't come for the religious elite, faultless, or morally perfect. He came for sinners like you and me, people who are culturally considered no better off than the shepherds in Jesus's time. That wasn't just any good news then—it's still the good news for *all* people *now*.

Thoughts about Advent

How does it make you feel that God goes out of His way to reveal great news to people who are overlooked? Considering how God is with us, how can we minister to people in our society this Christmas and reveal the heart of God?

_____

_____

_____

_____

_____

Day 22

The Savior—yes, the Messiah, the Lord—has been born today in Bethlehem, the city of David! And you will recognize him by this sign: You will find a baby wrapped snugly in strips of cloth, lying in a manger.

Luke 2:11–12

Every once in a while, my mind is blown away by Scripture. This passage falls into that category because Jesus, known as the Bread of Life, was born in Bethlehem, and Bethlehem means "the house of bread."[7] As a sign, the shepherds were told to look for a baby in a manger. Friend, that's a feeding trough for animals. So here we have the *Bread of Life*, born in *the House of Bread*, being revealed to the shepherds in a place *where animals go to eat*.

Jesus was not laid in that manger by accident. There was a crucial point God wanted to make. For you and me to survive, we hunger, we eat, we hunger again, we eat, and the cycle continues. But in order to fill our *spiritual hunger*, we require a different type of bread. We need a supernatural and eternal sustenance. This can only come to us from a supernatural source, Jesus.

Jesus confirmed God's great plan in John 6:32–37 when He described Himself, saying that God had given man true bread from heaven and that He was that true bread. His disciples still weren't exactly sure what He meant, as He explained that earthly sustenance would leave them longing for more, and that *He* was the food that would satisfy them for eternity.

Friend, Jesus knew we would hunger for many things. He knew we would, more often than not, look to the wrong things to satisfy those hungers. We hunger for money, thinking a full bank account will make us feel safe. We hunger for different social circles, thinking that who we know will help us feel secure. We hunger for control, thinking this is where we find respect. But the reality is, Jesus is the only One who can truly satisfy the hunger of our souls. He is the Bread of Life. True satisfaction will only come when we begin to feast upon Him.

Thoughts about Advent

Have you ever felt hungry for the things of this world? How have you tried to satisfy that hunger? What would it look like to give those earthly hungers to Jesus today? How can you feast upon the Bread of Life in your daily life?

_____

_____

_____

_____

_____

Day 23

Suddenly, the angel was joined by a vast host of others—the armies of heaven—praising God and saying, "Glory to God in highest heaven, and peace on earth to those with whom God is pleased."
Luke 2:13–14

Peace. We are a people that will seek peace at almost any cost.

We want world peace because we value peace.

World leaders engage in peace talks.

We try not to disrupt the peace.

The highest honor given to a peacemaker is called the Nobel Peace Prize.

So the question is, if we are so challenged to seek peace and so determined to maintain peace, how can we actually have it?

The answer is found in Jesus Christ.

The Greek word for *peace* in Luke 2 is *eirēnē* and stands for the peace that the Messiah brings.[8] It's the peace that comes by way of salvation resulting in our having peace with God. The angels were essentially saying, *You've been at war with God, but now there is a way to have peace with Him! Salvation has come! Peace has come!*

Interestingly, this translation also denotes wholeness. Apart from Jesus we are like a puzzle that is not complete yet. We were born missing that uniquely shaped piece that can only fit a certain way. This passage tells us that Jesus came to bring us peace, but more than that, He is the missing piece in the puzzle of our lives to make us whole.

Moreover, not only is Jesus the peace, *eirēnē*, we need to be reconciled to God, the One who restores us to wholeness, but He also offers us the gift of peace, *shalom* in Hebrew, for our own hearts and minds. Isaiah 48:18 says, "Oh, that you had listened to my commands! Then you would have had peace (*shalom*) flowing like a gentle river and righteousness rolling over you like waves in the sea."

Every Hebrew word conveys a feeling, an intent, and an emotion. There is not one English word that can completely encompass the Hebrew word for the kind of peace Jesus gifts when we enter into a relationship with Him. The word *shalom* describes more than just simply peace as we know it; it is a complete peace, a feeling of contentment, completeness, wholeness, well-being, and harmony. It means health, safety, soundness, tranquility, prosperity, perfectness, fullness, rest, harmony, and the complete absence of agitation or discord.[9]

Isaiah 9:6 tells us that Jesus would be the Prince of Peace. Jesus *is* our peace. He gives us both *eirēnē*, with God, and *shalom*, peace of mind. The reality is, we can seek what we consider peace all day long. We can travel to paradise destinations, turn off our cell phones, get away for a weekend of solitude, or try to escape in every other way to try and find peace. But the peace that we really need is only found in Christ Jesus. Friend, if you don't have the peace that Jesus brings, both *eirēnē* and *shalom*, then every other peace you seek will be futile. Jesus came to bring peace to earth. Invite His peace to rule your life today.

Thoughts about Advent

Considering that Christ came to bring both *eirēnē*, peace with God, and *shalom*, peace of mind, how have you applied that truth to your life? Do you have peace with God? Do you experience peace of mind? During this Advent season, how can you remind yourself that Jesus is your peace?

_____

_____

_____

_____

_____

_____

Day 24

When the angels had returned to heaven, the shepherds said to each other, "Let's go to Bethlehem! Let's see this thing that has happened, which the Lord has told us about." They hurried to the village and found Mary and Joseph. And there was the baby, lying in the manger. After seeing him, the shepherds told everyone what had happened and what the angel had said to them about this child. All who heard the shepherds' story were astonished.

Luke 2:15

The news was too great, they couldn't just stay in the fields! The shepherds had just heard the most incredible story in the most unimaginable way, and they had to see this holy baby for themselves. Upon observation, these men couldn't contain their discovery and had to share it with everyone they knew.

In a sense, many of us have symbolically traveled the same path as these shepherds. At one point, someone shared with us about Jesus who had brought them salvation. They shared with us how He had brought peace between themselves and God as well as peace of mind. Then we felt something rise up in our own souls. Could it be true for us as well? Would this Jesus they spoke about do for us as they claimed He had done for them? So we traveled on our own to the places we heard Christ was present and worked to explore His reality. Instead of traveling to Bethlehem, we traveled to a church. Instead of discovering Him in a manger, we met Him through the influence of someone's life.

Today the impact of Christ's birth remains something we must still investigate individually. We have all been invited to examine whether or not Christ's birth happened and consider what sort of impact that will have on our own lives.

The story of Christ's birth is still as astonishing today as it was back then. Just as the shepherds felt compelled to share their knowledge with everyone they knew, so many of us have felt the same urge. The story is too incredible, too miraculous, too life-changing to keep to ourselves.

Each of our journeys may look different, but our discovery of Christ's reality will be the same. Jesus was born. Salvation has come. Light has broken through. Hope has been restored, and now everything has changed. Jesus's birth and life remains a message that cannot be contained.

Thoughts about Advent

Have you researched the reality of Christ's birth for yourself? Have you discovered His goodness and felt compelled to share it with everyone you know? How can you share the good news of Jesus Christ with those around you during this Advent season?

_____

_____

_____

_____

_____

_____

Day 25

But Mary kept all these things in her heart and thought about them often. The shepherds went back to their flocks, glorifying and praising God for all they had heard and seen. It was just as the angel had told them.

Luke 2:19–20

A woman is a great protector of the sacred thoughts of her heart. We have the ability to pull up memories, emotions, and thoughts over any given matter at a moment's notice. I don't think it was any different for Mary. In fact, other versions of this passage of Scripture say that she "treasured, pondered, preserved, and kept thinking" about all the things that had happened in those nine short months.

It seems to me that over Jesus's lifetime, Mary would have recalled having her seemingly normal life interrupted by the most abnormal news. She would have remembered her angelic encounter and her immediate fear of what was happening to her. She was overcome by faith. I imagine she would have rehearsed Elizabeth's words regarding her as blessed among all women, especially when things got hard. I think she would have laughed over the insanity of her journey to Bethlehem on a donkey while nine months pregnant. Maybe she would have recalled the palpable fear of not having a place to bear her child and the exhausting labor of bringing a child into this world. I imagine her remembering the sight of the shepherds who would come to marvel over her son. I can see her wondering in awe as she caressed the tenderness of her newborn baby.

Friends, now that we have heard the story and have explored the news on our own, we must think of what this means to us personally. Jesus didn't come just to save Mary, Joseph, and the shepherds. Jesus came to bring salvation to you and me! And the best news? Jesus is coming again! And this time, it's not as a helpless baby born in a stable but as reigning King on a fiery, white horse commanding judgment (Matthew 25:31–33).

Friends, there are 318 references to Jesus's second coming in the New Testament; that's roughly one out of every thirteen verses. The Lord has gone out of His way to be clear that He is coming to make everything right again. Jesus's return means that all of the pain and suffering in our lives won't last forever. This is such a wonderful promise to those of us who await His second coming!

Everything the angel told Mary came true. Everything Jesus has told us is true. Let us fully embrace this truth into our lives this Christmas because now it is *our* time for us to glorify and praise God for everything we have now seen and heard!

Thoughts about Advent

Friends, this season of Advent is a perfect time to ponder these same matters in our own hearts. Are we continuously thinking of how different our lives will be because of the birth of this baby? Have we allowed the truth of God putting on human flesh to penetrate our hearts? How can we glorify God today for everything we have now seen and heard?

_____

_____

_____

_____

_____

_____

Notes

1. Interlinear Bible, as found at Bible Hub, https://biblehub.com/interlinear/luke/1-19.htm.

2. *Strong's Concordance*, as found at Bible Hub, from Luke 1:31, https://biblehub.com/greek/2424.htm.

3. Elizabeth Johnson, "Commentary on Luke 2:1–20," Working Preacher, December 24, 2011, https://www.workingpreacher.org/preaching.aspx?commentary_id=1157.

4. Wikipedia, https://en.wikipedia.org/wiki/Chronos and https://en.wikipedia.org/wiki/Kairos.

5. Ralph F. Wilson, "The Shepherds' Sign of the Manger (Luke 2:1-20)," *JesusWalk*, accessed October 19, 2020, http://www.jesuswalk.com/christmas-incarnation/shepherds-manger.htm.

6. Ralph F. Wilson, "Shepherds in Bethlehem (Luke 2:8–20)," *JesusWalk*, accessed October 19, 2020, http://www.jesuswalk.com/lessons/2_8-20.htm.

7. John Piper, "Bethlehem: House of Bread," *DesiringGod*, April 28, 1981, https://www.desiringgod.org/articles/bethlehem-house-of-bread.

8. *Strong's Concordance,* as found at Bible Hub, https://biblehub.com/greek/1515.htm.

9. *Strong's Concordance*, as found at Bible Hub, https://biblehub.com/hebrew/7965.htm.

ORDER INFORMATION

REDEMPTION
P R E S S

To order additional copies of this book, please visit
www.redemption-press.com.
Also available on Amazon.com and BarnesandNoble.com
Or by calling toll free 1-844-2REDEEM.

CPSIA information can be obtained
at www.ICGtesting.com
Printed in the USA
LVHW101527141122
733099LV00020B/211